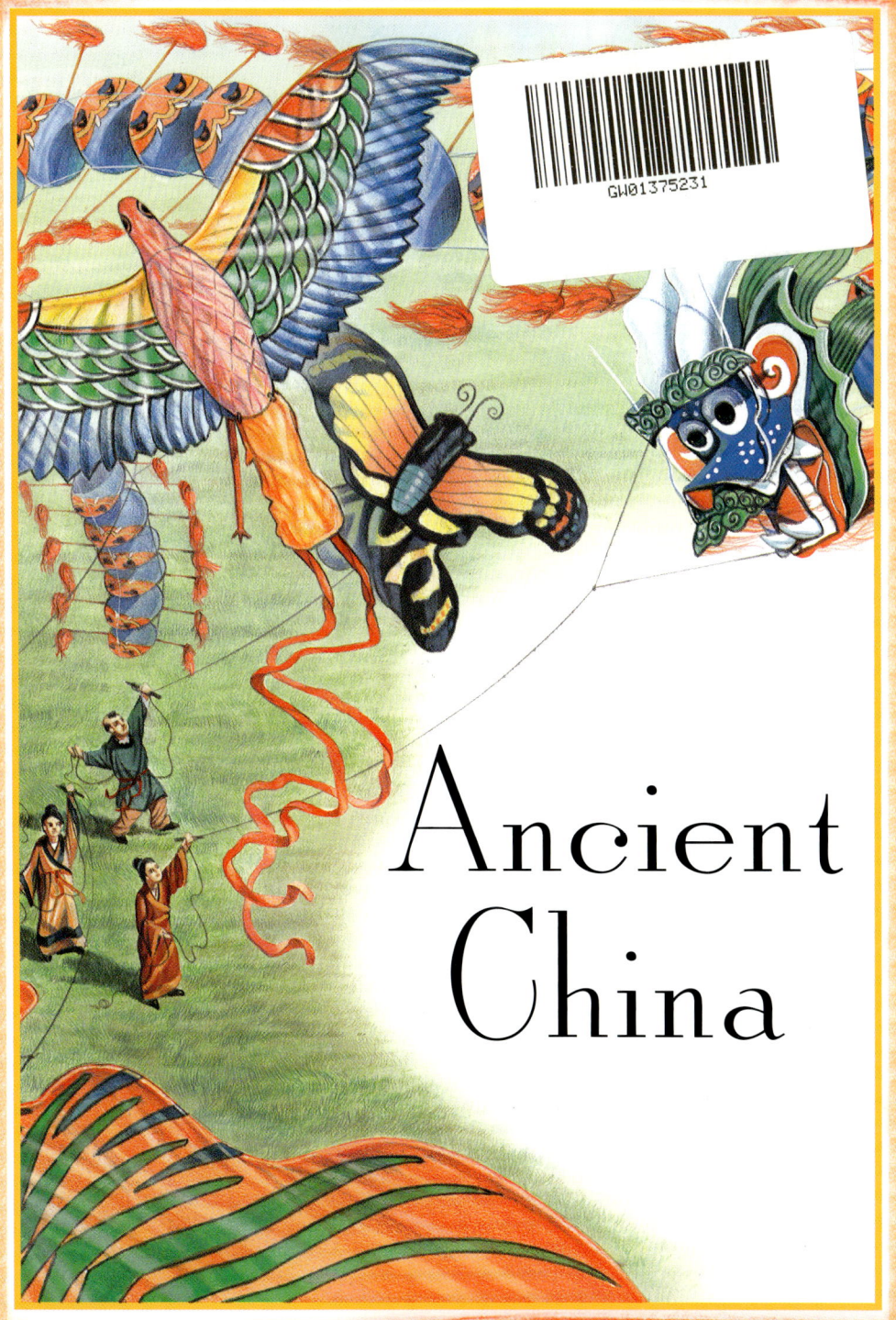

Ancient China

Contents

Ancient Beginnings	4
The Rule of Dynasties	6
Family Life	8
Fashion Statement	10
Time to Celebrate	12
War and Defence	
People of Power	14
The Long Wall	15
Canals and Camels	20
A Golden Time	22
The Written Word	24
Medicine and Learning	26
Practical Solutions	28
Glossary	30
Index	31
Research Starters	32

Features

Have you ever invented a new way of preparing a favourite food? Read on page 12 how a delicious recipe came about by accident.

The letters *A.D.* and *B.C.* are often used with dates. Find out the purpose of these letters on page 17.

Discover how we remember an emperor who lived over two thousand years ago. Turn to **A Silent Army** on page 18.

Who was the Italian traveller who wrote a book over 700 years ago about China? Find out on page 21.

Why were horses respected in China?

Visit **www.infosteps.co.uk**
for more about **ANCIENT CHINA**.

Ancient Beginnings

The civilization of ancient China began about 8,000 years ago when people settled along three great rivers—the Yellow River in the north, the Wei River in the northwest and the Yangtze River in the south. For hundreds of years the Chinese were cut off from other cultures by mountains, deserts and sea. They developed their own way of life and called their country "the Middle Kingdom" because they thought it was the centre of the universe. Emperors ruled the land for thousands of years.

Himalayan Mountains

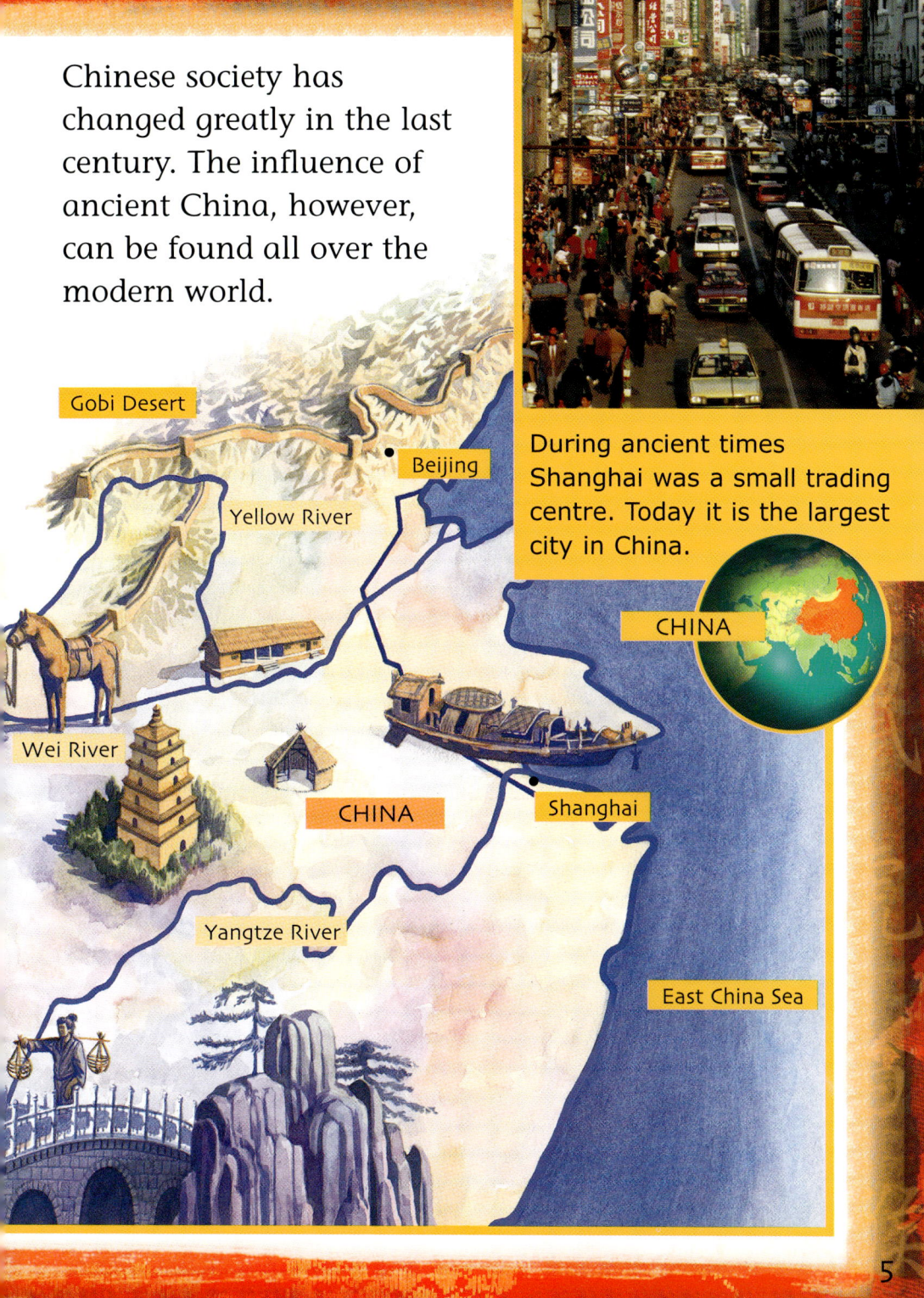

Chinese society has changed greatly in the last century. The influence of ancient China, however, can be found all over the modern world.

During ancient times Shanghai was a small trading centre. Today it is the largest city in China.

The Rule of Dynasties

Scholar

Peasant

Artisan

Merchant

For over 2,000 years China was ruled by families called **dynasties**. There were several great dynasties that lasted for hundreds of years. These ruling families were very rich. People believed that the head of the family, the emperor, received the power to rule from heavenly **ancestors**. He was called the "Son of Heaven".

IN FOCUS

Ancient Chinese society was like a ladder, with the emperor and his family at the top. Below them were the scholars who were highly respected for their ability to read and write. Below the scholars were peasants and **artisans**. Although the peasants were poor farmers China depended on them for food. The artisans made things people needed such as tools, pots and weapons.

The merchants were near the bottom of the ladder. They were looked down upon because they made nothing, yet often grew rich from trading goods.

During the Tang dynasty China was the greatest empire in the ancient world. An emperor would display his great wealth to important visitors from other lands.

Family Life

Several **generations** of Chinese families lived together in one house. The men were considered more important than the women. When a girl married she left her home and moved into the house of her husband and his family. Grandfathers and grandmothers were greatly respected. Children were expected to obey their parents and to look after them when they grew old. Poor families sometimes sold their daughters to be servants in the homes of wealthy people.

TIME LINK

Ancient Chinese names showed the importance of family. The family name was always written and spoken first and the personal name came last. Family is still very important in China today. Many Chinese people continue to give their family name first.

Wang Jia Li is the newest member of the Wang family. Her name, Jia Li, means "good and beautiful".

Fashion Statement

In ancient China clothing showed the **classes** of people and thus their places in society. The cloth, coloured with vegetable dyes, showed the wearer's importance. Only the emperor could wear yellow. Ordinary people dressed in blue or black. White was worn when someone died.

Fashions changed over the years, but women usually wore a long skirt and a jacket. Men wore loose robes with wide sleeves. Important people dressed in clothes of fine silk. Peasants wore a long shirt-like garment made of sacking that they could tuck up around their legs when they were working on the land.

> Fashionable women in the Tang dynasty wore flowing silk clothes. They arranged their hair in a topknot held in place with a comb or fancy pin.

A wealthy man's hat was an important part of his outfit. As the years passed hat fashions changed, with many styles being popular. Scholars' hats were made by folding cloth into a shape and then coating it with paint so that it kept the shape.

Emperor's hat

Warrior's helmet

Scholar's cage hat

IN FOCUS Women in ancient China developed the silk industry. They gathered mulberry leaves to feed caterpillars that spun cocoons made of silk. The cocoons were soaked in hot water to loosen the threads before the adult moths emerged.

Woven silk was very precious. Beautiful designs were **embroidered** and pictures were painted on it. Silk became an important trading item.

Scholar's turban

Scholar's kerchief hat

11

Time to Celebrate

A festival day was a time for families to come together to share food and fun. Many festivals still celebrated in China today date back to ancient times. The Spring Festival, for example, welcomed a new year in ancient China. People lit lanterns and exploded bamboo firecrackers. They ate specially prepared vegetable dishes, watched street entertainers and took part in ceremonies. Many of the wonderful recipes from ancient times are now enjoyed around the world.

TIME LINK

Beggar's Chicken is an ancient recipe that is still enjoyed today. The story is told that a poor peasant had just killed his chicken for cooking when he saw some soldiers approaching. He knew they might be hungry and eat his chicken so he quickly covered it in clay and threw it in the fire.

The soldiers sat by the peasant's fire for a long time enjoying its warmth. When they left, the peasant was so angry at having his meal burned that he struck the clay with a stick. The clay split open and the peasant could hardly believe his eyes. There was a beautifully cooked meal— Beggar's Chicken was invented.

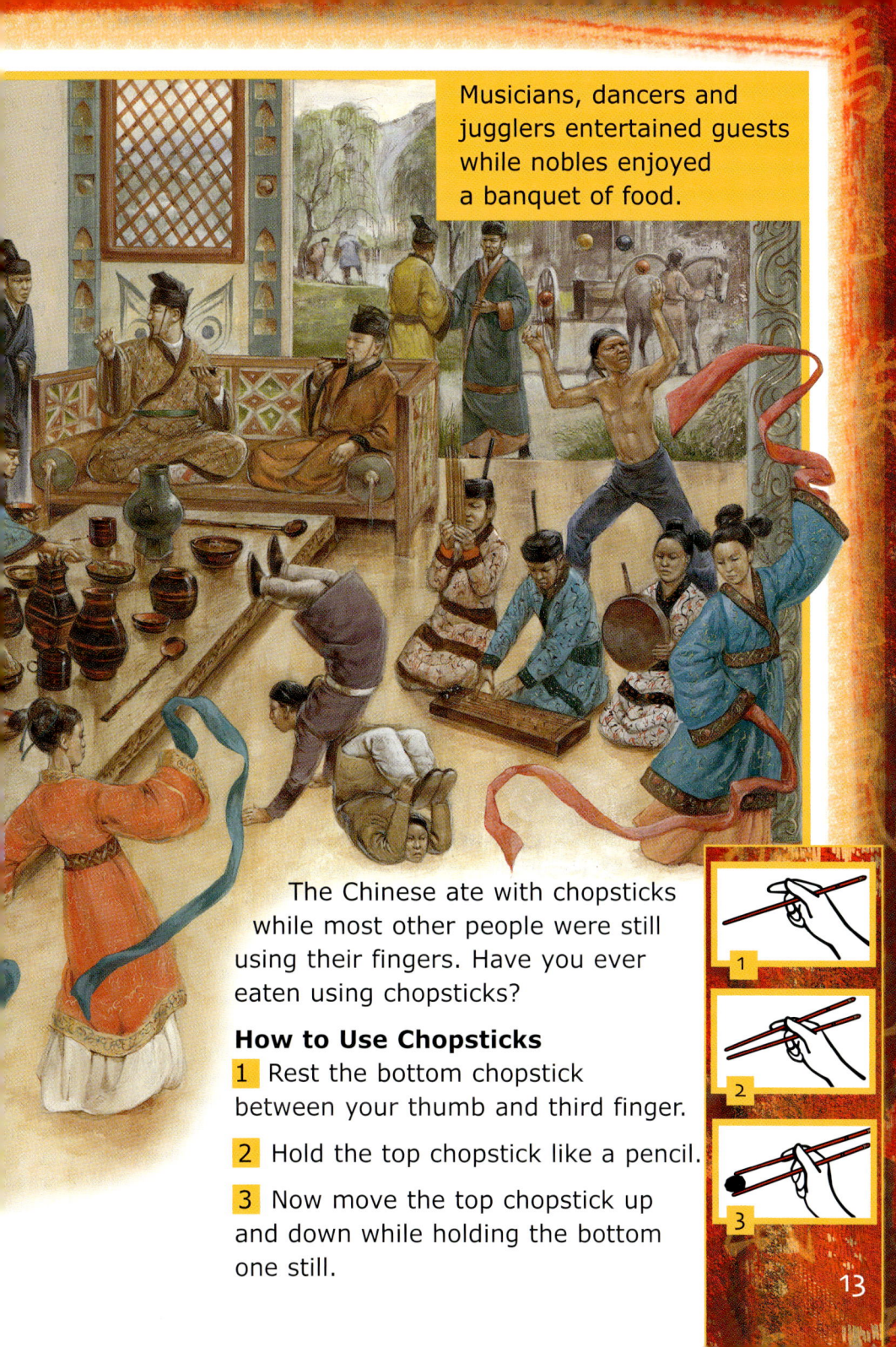

Musicians, dancers and jugglers entertained guests while nobles enjoyed a banquet of food.

The Chinese ate with chopsticks while most other people were still using their fingers. Have you ever eaten using chopsticks?

How to Use Chopsticks

1 Rest the bottom chopstick between your thumb and third finger.

2 Hold the top chopstick like a pencil.

3 Now move the top chopstick up and down while holding the bottom one still.

13

War and Defence

People of Power

Different groups of people lived in communities spread across the vast lands of China. Many of these groups fought each other for power and for the right to rule.

Nearly 2,000 years ago the warlike Zhou people from the Wei River valley began a dynasty that lasted more than 800 years. During the Zhou dynasty the kingdom expanded, cities grew in size and number and merchants began to trade between cities.

Why were horses respected in China?

Visit **www.infosteps.co.uk**
for more about **ANCIENT CHINA.**

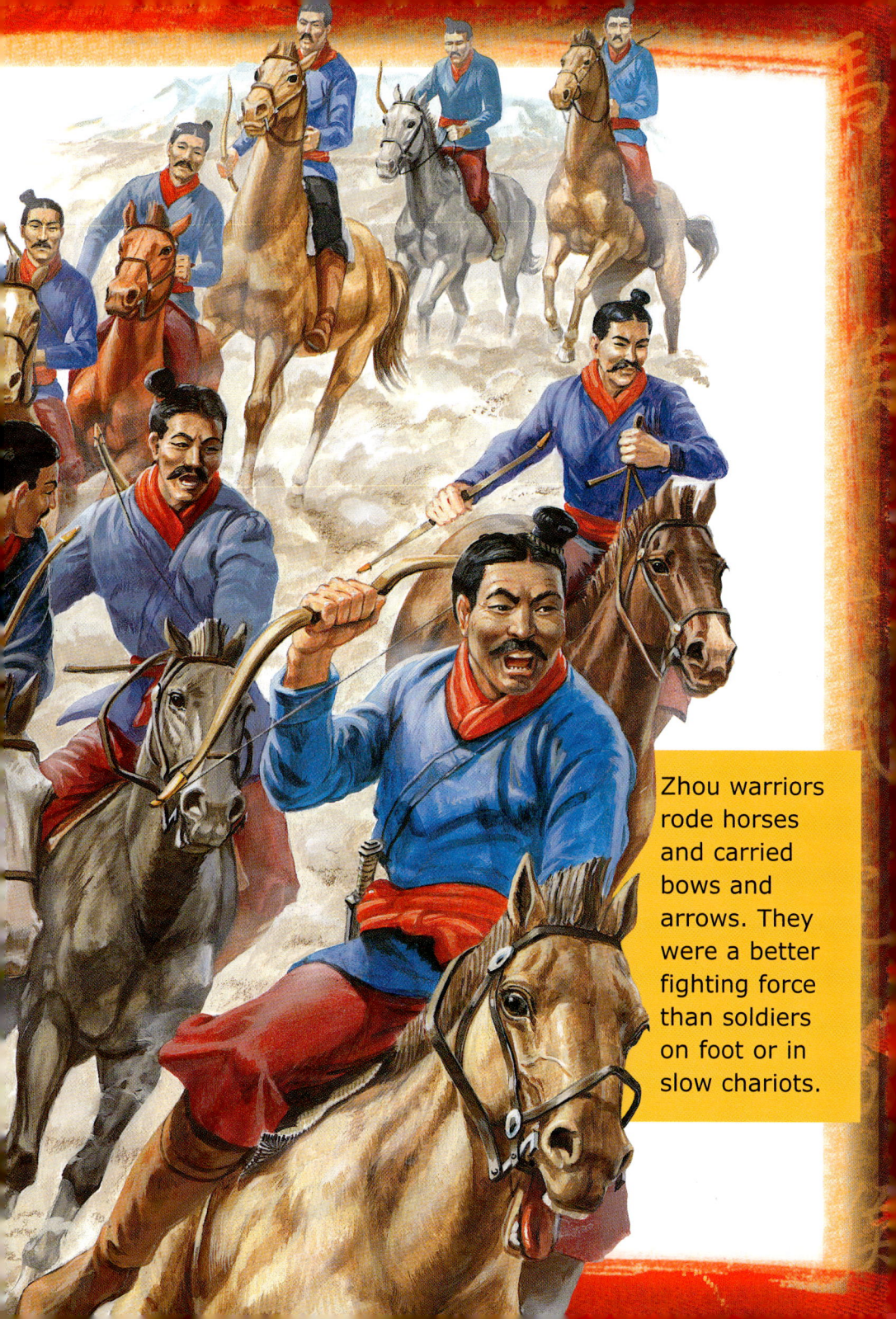

Zhou warriors rode horses and carried bows and arrows. They were a better fighting force than soldiers on foot or in slow chariots.

Canals and Camels

During the Han dynasty, which lasted over 400 years, the emperors strengthened the government and extended China's boundaries. Huge canals and roads were built linking cities and rivers. The inland waterways made trading, collecting taxes and transporting food much easier.

Many families lived on houseboats. Babies often had bamboo floats tied to their backs until they learned to swim.

Trade also grew along the famous Silk Road, linking Asia with Europe. Merchants formed camel caravans to protect themselves and their goods from robbers. The goods were sold from one caravan to the next until the cargo reached its market.

IN FOCUS

Marco Polo is one of the Silk Road's best known travellers. In 1271 he journeyed from Venice, Italy to China. He stayed in China for nearly 20 years.

When he returned to Italy he wrote a book called *Description of the World*. Marco Polo's writing gave early Europeans their first knowledge of China's advanced culture.

A Golden Time

The Tang dynasty ruled China for almost 300 years. This time was known as "a Golden Age". As trade routes expanded people from other lands visited China bringing new ideas and new ways of making things. During this time art, craft, music and literature developed. Clothing changed and new foods were introduced. Tea, grown in the warmer south, reached the markets in northern China and became a popular drink among the wealthy.

The Chinese artisans were skilled. They painted beautiful designs on silk and pottery and they carved bronze, jade and clay into works of art.

Jade was highly valued and was called the "stone of heaven". Dragons, which were considered to have special powers, often appeared in ancient Chinese art.

The market was a busy place where many languages were spoken. Musicians entertained shoppers and goods were loaded onto camels and into oxcarts.

The Written Word

Writing developed from very early times in ancient China. Before people had paper they wrote on thin bamboo strips, cutting characters for their words into the wood from top to bottom. Many of the early writings were government records. They are kept to this day.

A way of making paper was developed in China over 1,800 years ago. Bark, roots, rags and old fishing nets were pounded into a pulp and then dried on screens to make sheets of paper. During the Tang dynasty the Chinese also invented a way of printing by carving text and pictures onto wooden blocks. While European scholars were copying books by hand, the Chinese were inking wooden blocks and stamping them onto sheets of paper that were then stitched together to make books.

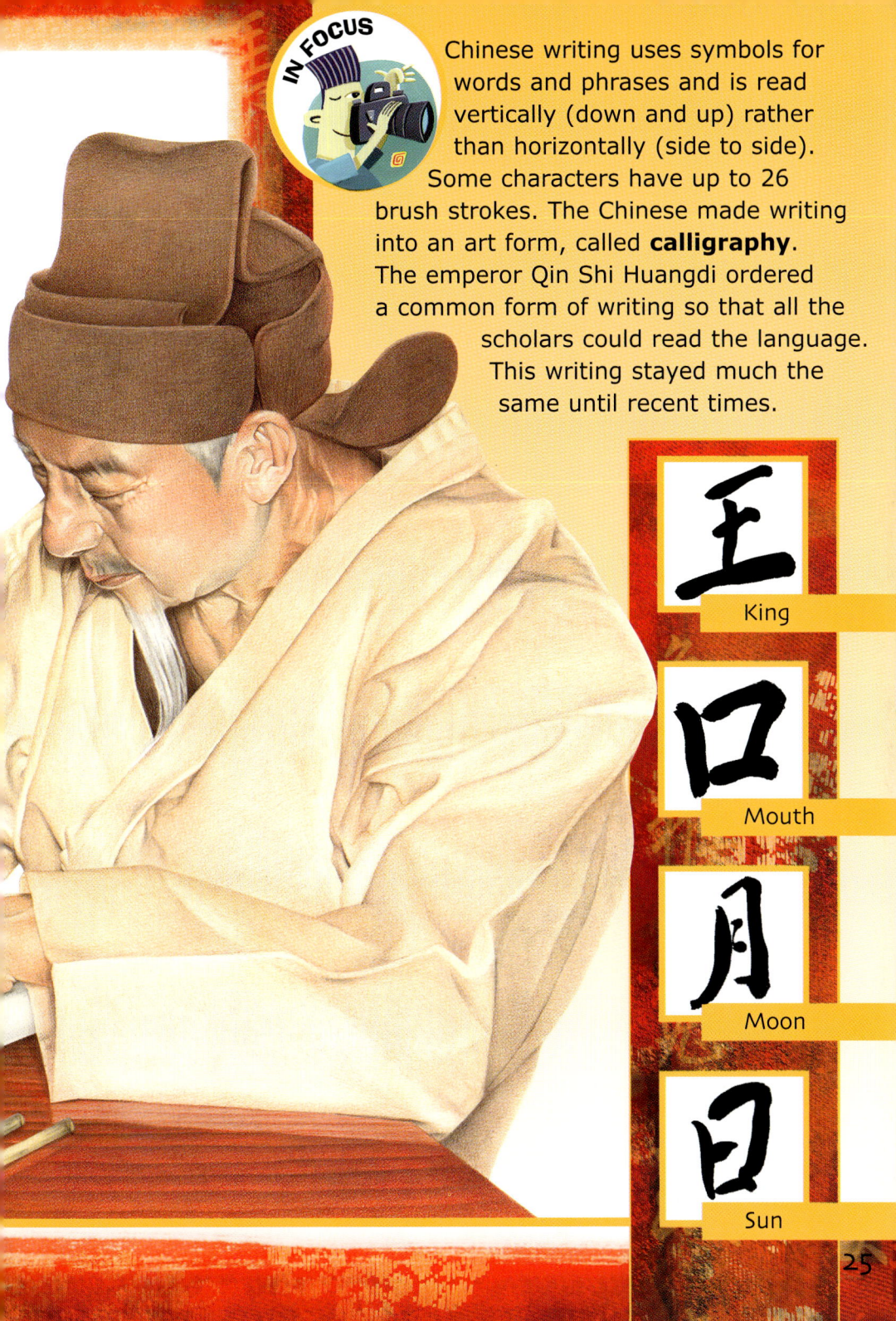

IN FOCUS

Chinese writing uses symbols for words and phrases and is read vertically (down and up) rather than horizontally (side to side). Some characters have up to 26 brush strokes. The Chinese made writing into an art form, called **calligraphy**. The emperor Qin Shi Huangdi ordered a common form of writing so that all the scholars could read the language. This writing stayed much the same until recent times.

王 King

口 Mouth

月 Moon

日 Sun

Medicine and Learning

The ancient Chinese believed that the body was a gift and must be cared for. Over thousands of years the ancient Chinese developed many ways to improve their health and care for sick people. These ways included **acupuncture**, exercise, massage and herbal medicine.

Ancient Chinese doctors used acupuncture, which involves placing needles into certain points on the body. Today acupuncture is practised in many parts of the world.

Ancient Chinese studies of medicine are the oldest in the world. As early as the Tang dynasty doctors had to pass regular exams to prove their knowledge. Practising medicine was honourable work for scholars, and it was one of the few professions women in ancient China could follow.

Coriander

Herbs were an important ingredient in ancient Chinese medicine. They were often used in teas or dried and combined with other herbs, leaves, roots and barks.

Garlic

Ginseng

Star Anise

Have you ever seen this symbol? This yin-yang symbol represents the ancient Chinese belief that the forces of nature balance each other. Many Chinese believe that for good health and happiness the body must have an equal balance of yin and yang forces.

Practical Solutions

The ancient Chinese were far ahead of the rest of the world in inventing practical ways to solve problems. Many of the tools and gadgets we use today were invented by the ancient Chinese. They developed wheelbarrows about 1,300 years before Europeans copied the idea. Their inventions of paper, printing, gunpowder and the compass made a great difference to our world. Other early Chinese inventions that we use today include matches, woks and mechanical clocks.

This compass has a wooden fish and a piece of metal floating in a bowl of water. We call it a compass, but the ancient Chinese called this invention a south-pointing fish.

Wheelbarrows were first used in China around A.D. 100.

28

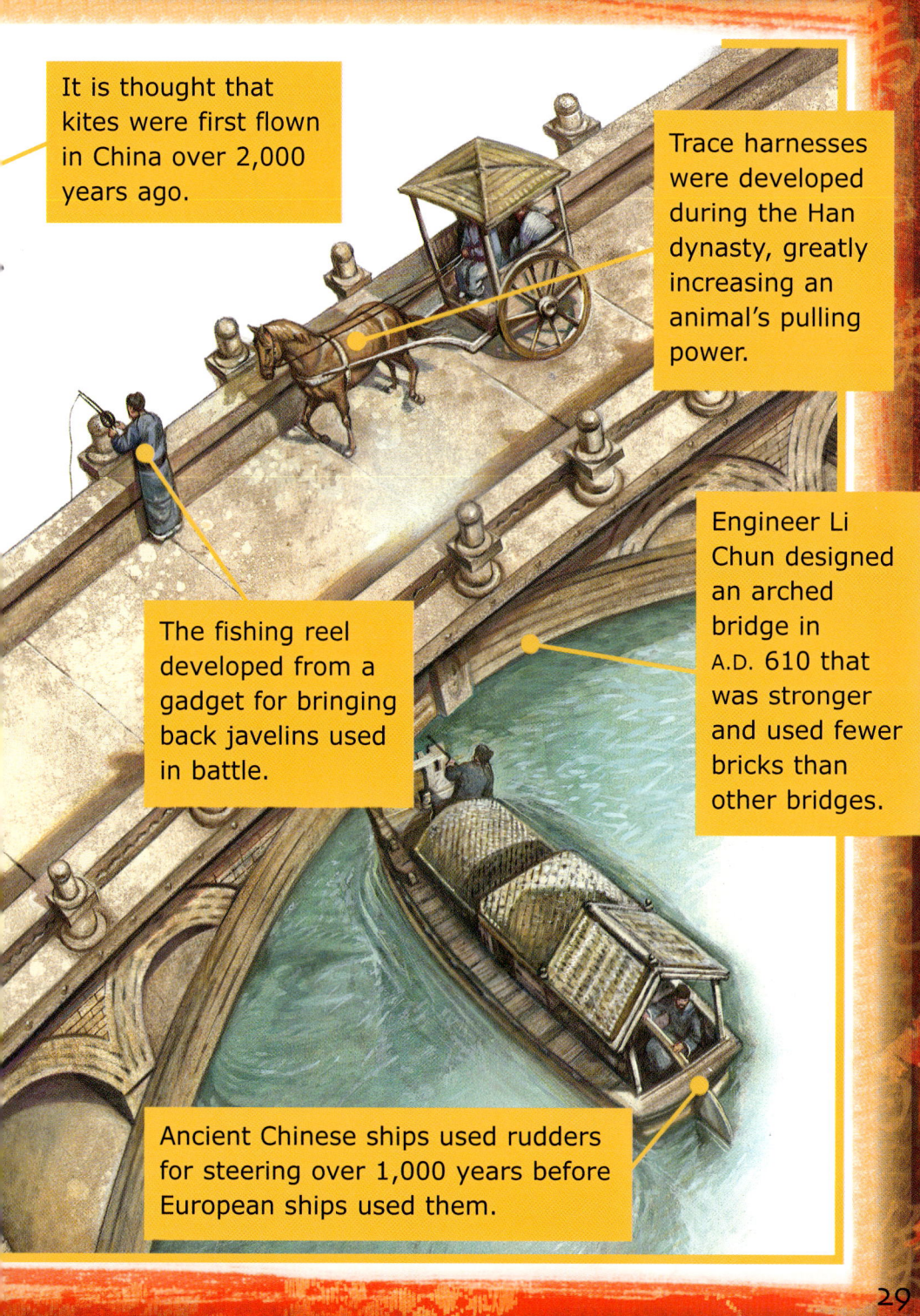

It is thought that kites were first flown in China over 2,000 years ago.

Trace harnesses were developed during the Han dynasty, greatly increasing an animal's pulling power.

The fishing reel developed from a gadget for bringing back javelins used in battle.

Engineer Li Chun designed an arched bridge in A.D. 610 that was stronger and used fewer bricks than other bridges.

Ancient Chinese ships used rudders for steering over 1,000 years before European ships used them.

29

Glossary

acupuncture – a Chinese method of easing pain or treating illness, first practised in ancient times. Needles are inserted under the skin at certain points on the body.

ancestor – someone in your family who lived a long time ago, usually before your grandparents

artisan – a person who is skilled at making things by hand. Carpenters and weavers are artisans.

calligraphy – the art of beautiful writing. Special brushes and inks are used in Chinese calligraphy.

class – a group of people, animals or things that are similar. A class of people have a similar way of life or income.

dynasty – a series of rulers who belong to the same family

embroider – to sew a design on cloth

generation – a single stage in the history of a family. A grandfather, mother and son are three generations. People who are born around the same time are also known as a generation, for example, "the younger generation".

Silk Road – the name given to the ancient trade route that crossed the Gobi Desert, linking China and Europe. The Silk Road became a highway for goods, ideas, information and skills.

terracotta – a hard, waterproof, brownish-red clay. The ancient Chinese made terracotta models and figures to place in tombs.

Index

acupuncture	26
artisans	6, 22
calligraphy	24–25
dynasties	6–7, 10, 14–17, 20, 22, 24, 29
emperors	4, 6–7, 10–11, 15, 18, 20, 25
Great Wall	15
inventions	24, 28–29
Long Wall	15–17
Marco Polo	21
merchants	6, 14, 21
Middle Kingdom	4
peasants	6, 10, 12
Qin Shi Huangdi	15, 18, 25
scholars	6, 11, 24–25, 27
silk	10–11, 22
Silk Road	16, 21
Spring Festival	12
terracotta warriors	18
Wei River	4–5, 14
Yangtze River	4–5
Yellow River	4–5

Research Starters

① The ancient Chinese gave the world many inventions. Which Chinese invention has had the greatest effect on your life?

② Today, as in ancient times, Chinese communities enjoy flying kites to celebrate festivals. During wartimes in ancient China kites were also used for another purpose. What else can you find out about kites?

③ The ancient Chinese made some remarkable scientific and technological discoveries. There have also been major scientific achievements by modern Chinese scientists. Research modern Chinese scientists who have won a Nobel prize.

④ Some recipes such as Beggar's Chicken are happy accidents. Other new recipes are developed through trial and error or imagination. Develop and write a new recipe to delight your friends.